Life in the Early Islamic World

Early Islamic Empires

Lizann Flatt

Crabtree Publishing Company

www.crabtreebooks.com

Life in the Early Islamic World

Author: Lizann Flatt
Publishing plan research and development:
  Sean Charlebois, Reagan Miller
  Crabtree Publishing Company
Editor-in-Chief: Lionel Bender
Editors: Simon Adams, Lynn Peppas
Proofreaders: Laura Booth, Wendy Scavuzzo
Editorial director: Kathy Middleton
Design and photo research: Ben White
Cover design: Katherine Berti
Production: Kim Richardson
Prepress technician: Katherine Berti
Print and production coordinator:
  Katherine Berti
Maps: Stefan Chabluk

Consultants:
  Barbara Petzen, Founder, Middle East Connections
  and President, Middle East Outreach Council.

Cover: Map of the Umayyad Caliphate in 750 C.E. (top);
  Scene from the battle defending Constantinople,
  Paris, in 1499 (bottom right); image of Tariq ibn Ziyad
  (bottom left)
Title page: A Bedouin nomad in the Arabian Desert

Photographs and reproductions:
cover: Wikimedia Commons: Courtesy of The General
  Libraries, The University of Texas at Austin: cover (top),
  www.greece.org/Romiosini/fall.html: cover (bottom
  right), Theodor Hosemann (1807-1875): cover (bottom left)
interior: The Art Archive: 10 (British Library); Getty Images:
  11 (Dea Picture Library/De Agostini), 18–19 (Edinburgh
  University Library), 27 (Bibliothèque des Arts Décoratifs
  Paris/Gianni Dagli Orti), 28 (British Library), 30 (Bodleian
  Library Oxford), 32–33 (Bodleian Library Oxford), 39t
  (Bibliothèque Municipale Besançon/Kharbine-Tapabor/
  Coll. Jean Vigne), 39b (Museo Correr Venice/Collection
  Dagli Orti), 40 (Topkapi Museum Istanbul/Gianni
  Dagli Orti); shutterstock.com: 1 (berna namoglu), 3
  (Brian Chase), 4–5 (Attila Jandi), 6 (Jeffrey Liao), 12–13
  (Valery Shanin), 13t (Mihai-Bogdan Lazar), 15 (I. Pilon),
  17 (ollirg), 18 (Patrick Wang), 28–29 (Barbara Barbour),
  31 (David Evison), 32–33 (arazu), 36 (szefei), 36–37
  (Hector Conesa); Topfoto (The Granger Collection): 9,
  24, 35, 41, 43; 8, 14 (Topham Picturepoint), 19 (Roger-
  Viollet), 21b (The Print Collector/HIP), 21t (The Image
  Works), 22 (World History Archive), 23 (British Library
  Board/Robana), 25, 35 (HIP)

This book was produced for Crabtree Publishing
Company by Bender Richardson White.

Library and Archives Canada Cataloguing in Publication

Flatt, Lizann
    Early Islamic empires / Lizann Flatt.

(Life in the early Islamic world)
Includes index.
Issued also in electronic formats.
ISBN 978-0-7787-2171-0 (bound).--ISBN 978-0-7787-2178-9 (pbk.)

    1. Islamic Empire--History--Juvenile literature. 2. Iran--History--
Safavid dynasty, 1501-1736--Juvenile literature. 3. Turkey--History--
Ottoman Empire, 1288-1918--Juvenile literature. 4. Islam--History--
Juvenile literature. I. Title. II. Series: Life in the early Islamic world

DS38.3.F53 2013   j909'.09767   C2012-907293-1

Library of Congress Cataloging-in-Publication Data

Flatt, Lizann.
    Early Islamic empires / Lizann Flatt.
      p. cm. -- (Life in the early Islamic world)
    Includes index.
    ISBN 978-0-7787-2171-0 (reinforced library binding : alk. paper) --
ISBN 978-0-7787-2178-9 (pbk. : alk. paper) -- ISBN 978-1-4271-9838-9
(electronic pdf) -- ISBN 978-1-4271-9564-7 (electronic html)
1. Islamic Empire--History--Juvenile literature. 2. Iran--History--
Safavid dynasty, 1501-1736--Juvenile literature 3. Turkey--History--
Ottoman Empire, 1288-1918--Juvenile literature. 4. Islam--History--
Juvenile literature I. Title.

    DS37.7.F53 2013
    909'.09767--dc23
                                              2012043534

Crabtree Publishing Company

www.crabtreebooks.com   1-800-387-7650

Printed in Hong Kong/012013/BK20121102

Copyright © **2013 CRABTREE PUBLISHING COMPANY.** All rights reserved. No part of this publication may be reproduced, stored in a retrieval
system or be transmitted in any form or by any means, electronic, mechanical, photocopying, recording, or otherwise, without the prior written
permission of Crabtree Publishing Company. In Canada: We acknowledge the financial support of the Government of Canada through the Canada
Book Fund for our publishing activities.

Published in Canada
Crabtree Publishing
616 Welland Ave.
St. Catharines, Ontario
L2M 5V6

Published in the United States
Crabtree Publishing
PMB 59051
350 Fifth Avenue, 59th Floor
New York, New York 10118

Published in the United Kingdom
Crabtree Publishing
Maritime House
Basin Road North, Hove
BN41 1WR

Published in Australia
Crabtree Publishing
3 Charles Street
Coburg North
VIC, 3058

Contents

About This Book

Islam is the religion of Muslim people. Muslims believe in one God. They believe that the prophet Muhammad is the messenger of God. Islam began in the early 600s C.E. in the Arabian peninsula, in a region that is now the country of Saudi Arabia. From there, it spread across the world. Today, there are about 1.5 billion Muslims. About half of all Muslims live in southern Asia. Many Muslims also live in the Middle East and Africa, with fewer in Europe, North America, and Australia.

The Early Islamic World—Early Islamic Empires looks at how the Muslim community set up by Muhammad eventually spread to reach parts of North Africa, Europe, and Asia. It describes how many different but related Islamic empires were won and lost, and highlights the people who ruled them.

In the Beginning

Islam is a religion that governs many aspects of life for its followers, who are known as Muslims. **It was founded by the prophet Muhammad, who lived from 570 to 632** C.E. **Islam spread quickly from its beginnings in** Arabia. **Muslim rulers took over many lands throughout the Middle East, Asia, and North Africa.**

Below: The Great **Mosque** in Damascus, Syria, is one of the oldest examples of Islamic architecture. It was built about 715 C.E. during the Umayyad Dynasty so it is sometimes called the Umayyad Mosque.

A Multicultural Empire

The region of the world that was ruled by the first Muslim leaders is now known as the Early Islamic **Empire**. The empire changed and was split up over time as lands were conquered or lost. Within the growing Islamic world, there were many separate regions with people with different **cultures**, languages, and beliefs, but their leaders all followed the religion of Islam.

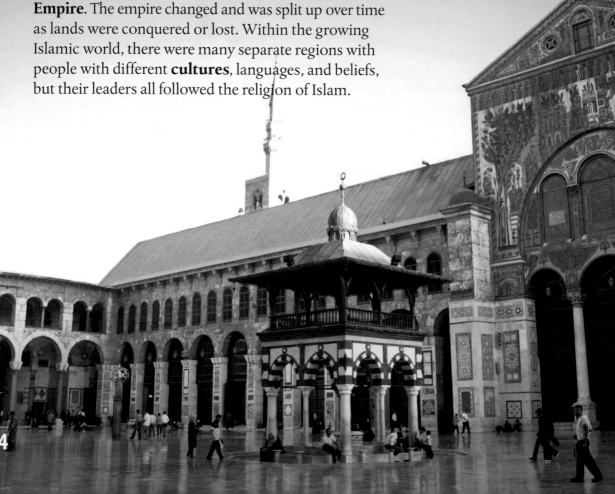

Muslim Society

Leadership of a people was often passed from father to son and, in this way, power stayed within a family for several years. This system of leadership is called a **dynasty**.

Muslim rulers introduced their Islamic beliefs when they conquered other lands and cities. The rulers needed places to worship so they built mosques, and they constructed other buildings to support their government and ways of life. These buildings included palaces, communual baths, *bazaars*—which are marketplaces— and *madrasas*, or houses of learning. Many people in the conquered lands also took up the Islamic faith.

The Early Islamic Empire began in the desertlike region of Arabia and spread out to reach parts of present-day Spain, India, Russia, and Morocco. As Muslims came into contact with other cultures, they brought back items of value such as silk, spices, porcelain, and **textiles** from China and the Far East. They **traded** these goods with Europe in the west. Muslim scholars **translated** Ancient Greek and Latin manuscripts into Arabic, then built upon what they learned to create many new advances in science, medicine, and art.

Timeline

570–632 Muhammad's lifetime

632–661 Rule of the first four **caliphs**

661–750 Umayyad Dynasty

711 Start of the Islamic conquest of Spain and Portugal

749–1258 Abbasid Dynasty

909–1171 Fatimids rule North Africa, Egypt, and Syria

1050–1147 Almoravids rule North Africa and Spain

1071 Seljuk Turks defeat the **Byzantines**

1096–1099 First **Crusade** by Christian armies against Muslim states in Palestine

1171–1250 Ayyubids rule Egypt and Syria (Saladin is their most famous ruler)

1250–1517 Mamluks rule Egypt and Syria

1299–1918 **Ottoman** Empire

1370–1507 Timurid Dynasty in Iran

1501–1722 Safavids rule Iran

1526–1857 **Mughal** Empire in India

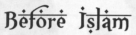

Camels

The camel was an important animal in the Early Islamic Empire. It was used to carry goods long distances so food or valuables could be traded across the empire. Processions of camels and traders were known as **caravans**. Warriors also rode camels in battles. In dry desert regions, camels can go for up to 17 days without water and weeks without food. They are strong and fast animals. People can drink camel's milk, burn camel dung for fuel, and make cloth or rope from the hair of camels.

Above: These remains of the ancient city of Petra in Syria date from about 100 B.C.E. The city was built by the Nabataeans, an Arab tribe influenced by Greek and Roman cultures.

Before Islam

In Arabia there were many tribes, or family groups, before the Islamic Empire. The people were Arabs—that is, they spoke Arabic. Most were also nomads, which means they traveled from place to place within a large territory. The nomads were called Bedouins. Some Arabs lived in cities, including a tribe called the Quraysh. They were the leaders of the city of Mecca, which was founded about 400 C.E.

Most pre-Islamic Arabians believed in many local gods with one supreme god above the others (**Allah**). There were some Arabs who followed Christianity and Judaism, mostly living in the far north of the peninsula and in some oasis towns such as Yathrib (later known as Medina).

To the north and west of Arabia was the Byzantine Empire. This was originally the eastern part of the Roman Empire. In the mid-400s, it separated from the western part of the Roman Empire, which then fell into decline. The Byzantine Empire was mostly Christian and spoke the Greek language. Its center of power was Constantinople (now Istanbul).

To the northeast of Arabia, the **Sasanid**, or **Persian**, Empire was ruled by the Sasanian Dynasty. The main religion here was Zoroastrianism, named for the prophet Zoroaster (also sometimes called Zarathustra). This religion has two gods or deities. It is based on the idea of the struggle between good and evil. Followers believe a creator made all good things and an evil figure tries to destroy them.

Heartland of the Empire

This map shows how the Early Islamic Empire had begun in the towns of Mecca and Medina in 632 C.E. and how it then spread quickly across the rest of Arabia to Europe by about 750. The Byzantine Empire, based in Constantinople, ruled most of the Mediterranean lands in Muhammad's time. The Sasanians ruled what are now Iran and Iraq from their capital, Ctesiphon (near Baghdad).

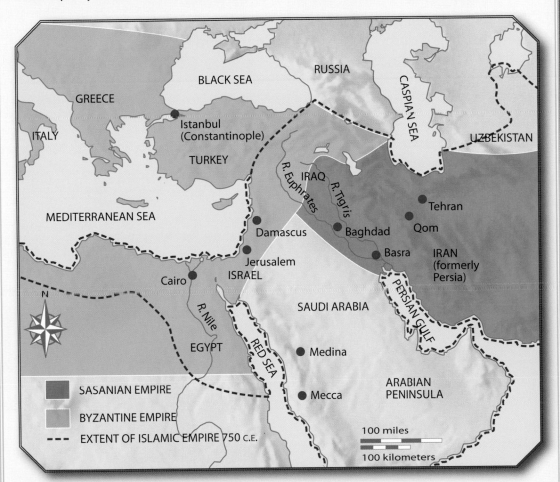

After 750 Muslim armies then took Islam to many distant lands. Parts of the Byzantine Empire in Western Asia and North Africa were conquered, along with the Sasanian or Persian Empire to the east. Both ancient empires were later overthrown by Muslim armies but only after many major battles and wars.

The Empire Grows

Muhammad was born in 570 to a poor branch of the ruling Quraysh tribe in Mecca. When he was 40, he began to receive and pass on messages that he believed were the word of Allah, an Arabic word for "the god." Islam grew first among a small group of his family and friends, but had become the main religion of Arabia by 632.

Below: This miniature painting from a book from the 1700s shows Muhammad praying for rain before the Battle of Badr.

Mecca to Medina

Muhammad believed in a single deity or god. The rulers of Mecca were pagans, who believed in many gods. They felt threatened by Muhammad's new religion because they thought the annual **pilgrimage** to the *Kaaba*, a holy monument, would lose importance. The Kaaba was visited by many people because it held many idols, or images or statues of gods, and this created a great deal of trade that the Quraysh did not want to lose. In 622, the Quraysh forced Muhammad to leave Mecca. Muhammad and his followers moved to Yathrib, which was renamed Medina.

In Medina, Muhammad began a new community of Muslims made of his followers from Mecca and new supporters from Medina. He worked as a judge to help settle disputes between people in Medina. The Muslims raided caravans from Mecca to get the food and goods they needed to live on. These raids angered the rulers of Mecca. Muslims still resented being forced

from their Mecca homes. Fights between the Quraysh of Mecca and the Muslims of Medina continued.

Battle of Badr

In 624, Muhammad lured a large camel caravan to Badr by filling wells along the caravan route with sand, forcing the caravan to stop at Badr to get water. The large army from Mecca that was accompanying the caravan clashed with Muhammad's smaller army. Muhammad's army won. This victory was seen by the Muslim followers as proof that Allah was behind them and is one of the most important victories in Muslim history.

Muhammad convinced many tribal leaders in the area to **convert** to Islam. With their help, his army marched into Mecca in 630. It took control and ordered all pagan idols to be removed from the Kaaba, which was then given over to Islam. Mecca became Muslim, and soon Muhammad had united much of the region under the Islamic faith. Religion replaced tribal loyalty as the main bond for people in the area. Jews and Christians in the region accepted Muhammad's rule and he allowed them to practice their own religion.

In 632, Muhammad became ill and died. Although he had many wives, his only surviving child was his daughter, Fatima. With no male to inherit Muhammad's leadership, his followers could not agree on a new leader. This caused a split within Islam.

Below: This miniature painting from 1237 shows a caravan of pilgrims going to Mecca. The pilgrimage, or *hadj*, is an important rite in Islam.

Islamic Calendar

The Islamic calendar, called the Hijri calendar, is different from the calendar used in the West (the solar Gregorian calendar). It begins with Muhammad's journey to Medina, called the *Hijra*. It is a lunar calendar, with either 29 or 30 days in a month, according to the Moon's cycle. A 12-month year in the Hijri calendar is about 11 days shorter than the solar year, so Islamic holy days move earlier through the seasons each year.

Jizya

When Muslims conquered a city they charged a *jizya* tax on all non-Muslims. If the non-Muslims paid this tax, they could continue to practice their own religion. This money was an important source of income for the Islamic Empire. Muslims also did not require Christians and Jews to convert to Islam because the Quran forbade it.

Above: This small painting shows the Battle of Qadisiyya in 634 between the Sasanids and the Muslim Arabs. Muslims were able to conquer the Sasanid Empire partly because the Sasanids were weakened from fighting the Byzantine Empire.

Caliphs Carry On

The Muslim community chose one of Muhammad's fathers-in-law, Abu Bakr, as the first caliph, or successor. This created a disagreement among Muslims. Those who agreed with this choice are today called Sunni Muslims. Those who thought Muhammad had wanted his son-in-law Ali to be the next leader are today called Shii Muslims.

Abu Bakr, who ruled from 632 to 634, faced a tribal revolt called the Ridda. With Muhammad gone, the tribes felt they no longer owed any loyalty to the Islamic state. In 633, the Ridda was defeated and the Arabian peninsula became Muslim.

The tribes were now united under Islam so they could no longer raid one another. Instead, Abu Bakr declared *jihad* —the struggle to defend Islam from unbelievers—against the neighboring Sasanid and Byzantine empires. Umar, the second caliph (634–644), expanded his rule beyond the Arabian peninsula. He captured the cities of Jerusalem in Palestine and Damascus in Syria from the Byzantines. His armies fought the Sasanids and, in 636, won the Battle of Qadisiyya near the Euphrates River. Then he moved farther east to capture the Sasanid capital, Ctesiphon. He also won lands in Egypt. Umar was killed in 644.

Disagreements

Uthman, the third caliph (644–656), made raids into North Africa. He built a fleet of naval ships to guard against the Byzantines on the Mediterranean Sea, and finished taking over the Sasanid Empire in 653. He appointed his Umayyad relatives—a branch of the Quraysh tribe—to positions of power within the government,. This was not a popular decision and, in 656, he was assassinated.

Ali was declared the fourth caliph (656–661) helped by his supporters. He was challenged by Muawiyah, however, who was governor of Syria and an Umayyad cousin of Uthman. Muhammad's friends, Talha and Zubair, and one of his widows, Aisha, also challenged Ali. A **civil war** was fought for years. At the Battle of the Camel in 656, both Talha and Zubair were killed and Aisha was taken prisoner. Ali was assassinated in 661. Muawiyah claimed the leadership.

Above: An embossed silver plate shows a Sasanid king hunting on horseback.

The Umayyads

The Umayyads arranged that leadership of their people passed to a male in the family. The capital was moved from Mecca to Damascus in Syria. The empire expanded into North Africa, Spain, and Central Asia. The Umayyads stayed in power for almost 100 years.

Unrest and Civil War

As Muawiyah expanded his empire, he moved the capital to the more central position of Damascus. He also forced many of the nomadic tribes to join his army, making them easier to control. When Muawiyah appointed his son Yazid the next caliph, many Muslims were angered because it took away their ability to elect their own leader. The Shii Muslims rebelled. They wanted Husayn, who was Ali's second son and Muhammad's grandson, to be caliph. Yazid's army defeated Husayn's army in the Battle of Karbala. Husayn was killed. His death shocked many Muslims, and widened the Sunni and Shii Muslim split.

Yazid died after only a few years in power, then so did his son. A cousin, Marwan, took over. Then his son Abd al-Malik ruled from 685 to 705. During this time, the second Islamic civil war took place, a series of rebellions by different groups, all of whom had their own leaders they wanted to replace the Umayyads. Abd al-Malik finally won out and established peace by 692. He made Arabic the official language of all government functions, and built the Dome of the Rock (see opposite).

Expanding the Empire

To the west of Arabia, the Umayyads gained the loyalty of the Berbers—several tribes of North Africans—and took lands from the Byzantines that are now the countries of Libya, Tunisia, Algeria, and Morocco. In 675, Kairouan in Tunisia became the Arab base in Africa and an important city in the Islamic Empire.

In 711, the Berber general Tariq led Muslim forces into the Iberian Peninsula, which is now the territories of Spain and Portugal. There he conquered the Christian **Visigoth** tribes. Tariq's forces even won lands in parts of present-day France but they were stopped by the Franks, a group from Germany, at the Battle of Poitiers in 732. The Umayyads called this new province al-Andalus and made Cordoba its capital city in 717.

To the east, Muslims wanted a route to China and the profitable trade that could be had there. In 715, they took the cities of Bukhara and Samarkand. This brought

Islam to the Turkish communities there. To the south, Muslims also invaded Sindh in 712. From there, they would later move farther into India.

The difference in wealth and opportunity between the ruling Arab Umayyads and regular citizens, especially the *mawali* (non-Arab Muslims), created unrest. In 749, groups of citizens together took power from the Umayyads. They made the next caliph Abu al-Abbas, a descendant of Muhammad's uncle, starting the Abbasids.

Mawali Muslims

The mawali were non-Arab Muslims (Persians, Egyptians, Turks, Berbers) who converted to Islam but did not have full Umayyad citizen rights. The mawali could not hold positions in government, had to pay the nonbeliever tax even though they were Muslim, and could not join the military. They fought to change this.

Above: The Dome of the Rock in Jerusalem, finished in 691 under the rule of Abd al-Malik, shows Byzantine influences in the shape of the dome.

Below: The now-ruined city of Jiaohe in China was a trading center for caravans. In Umayyad times, a Muslim community was located there.

The Abbasids

The Abbasids reorganized the Islamic Empire and promised equality for all Muslims. They supported the arts and sciences. They created a wealthy and powerful empire, but rival states also broke off to challenge them. The Abbasids ruled for more than 500 years.

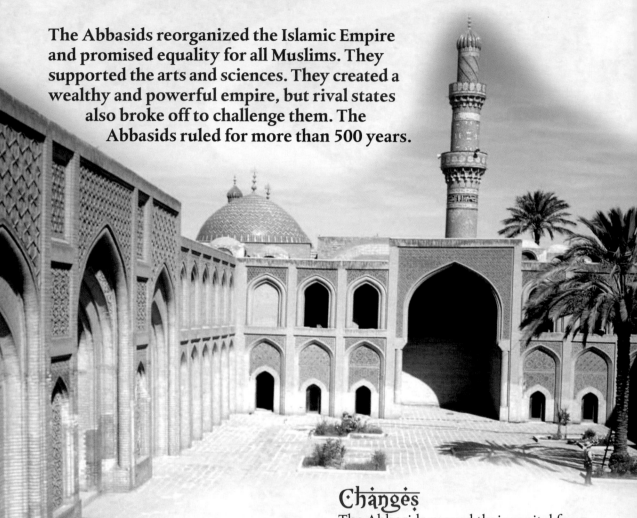

Above: The Mustansiriya madrasa in Baghdad became the most important university in Abbasid times. It was built under the direction of Caliph al-Mustansir Billah in 1227.

Changes

The Abbasids moved their capital from the former Umayyad capital of Damascus in Syria to a new city, Baghdad in Iraq, in 762. Persian mawali were brought into many government positions, including as *viziers*, or advisors to the caliphs, and as scholars in the House of Wisdom (see opposite).

Over time, the Abbasid caliphs began to lose control of the empire. The Buyids, a Persian-speaking dynasty, took effective control over the government in 945, although they kept the caliph in place as a figurehead, or leader in name only.

Below: This coin, a silver *dirham*, was used in the Abbasid dynasty from 786 to 809.

House of Wisdom

In the 800s, the Abbasids established a library and translation school in Baghdad. Scholars translated and interpreted great works of other cultures such as the writings of Plato and Aristotle. Muslims also made their own discoveries in many fields: medicine, arithmetic, geography, chemistry, and astronomy. Scholars from many lands came to study and learn and much knowledge was exchanged.

Other Rivals

Abd al-Rahman, the grandson of one of the former Umayyad caliphs, had escaped during the Abbasid takeover and fled to al-Andalus, in modern Spain. He took control of the city of Cordoba and made it his capital. He set up a government in the Umayyad name, claiming himself *emir*, or ruler, independent of the Abbasids.

In North Africa, the Aghlabid Dynasty ruled from their capital Fez (in present-day Morocco) under the Abbasid name, but they operated independently. In 909, the Fatimid Dynasty took power from them in North Africa and went on to take control of Egypt from the Abbasids in the 960s. The Fatimids, who were Shii, claimed they ruled all the Islamic Empire.

Meanwhile, in the east, Turkish tribal groups were moving from Central Asia into the Middle East. A Turkish dynasty, the Ghaznavids, created a new state in eastern Iran, Afghanistan, and northern India. They were soon challenged by another Sunni Turkish group, the Seljuks, who continued conquering to the west. The Seljuks defeated the Buyids and took control of Baghdad in 1050. Their leader, Togrul Beg, allowed the Abbasid caliph to stay in office but was made *sultan*—a Muslim king—and acted as leader. The Seljuk armies also defeated the Fatimids in Syria, then the Byzantines, opening that area to settlement by the Turkish tribespeople. The Abbasid caliphate came to an end in 1258, when the Mongols from China took over Baghdad.

The Seljuk Turks

The Seljuk sultans greatly helped the spread of Islam by defeating the Christian Byzantines, but they also attacked Shii Islamic dynasties to try to unite the empire under Sunni rule. Their victories allowed the large movement of Turkish peoples into new lands.

The Seljuk Family

The Seljuks were peoples of Turkish background. They converted to Sunni Islam and attracted other Turkish tribes of Central Asia to come under their leadership. The Seljuks led by Togrul Beg and his brother Chaghri Beg defeated the Ghaznavids and continued west. Many Turkish tribes followed them from Central Asia to settle in the Middle East. In 1055, Togrul Beg's forces marched into Baghdad and defeated the Buyids, who were Shii Muslims. They took over power in Baghdad, controlling the Abbasid caliph. Togrul sent other Seljuk family members to rule in new lands they conquered. Eventually the Seljuks were in positions of power in many parts of the Islamic world. Togrul Beg died in 1063.

Below: This painting from about 1300 shows Seljuk cavalry (on the right) fighting Mongol warriors (on the left).

Other Seljuk Conquests

Togrul's nephew Alp Arslan led the Seljuks to victory over the Byzantines in the Battle of Manzikert in 1071. He captured the Byzantine emperor and forced him to allow the Turks to move into their lands. Also in 1071, another Seljuk army took Jerusalem from the Fatimids.

After Alp Arslan was killed in 1073, his son Malikshah made Isfahan the dynasty's capital. Malikshah further expanded the empire but, after his death in 1092, the Seljuk dynasty began to break apart as various leaders wanted power. The Seljuks continued to battle against the Byzantines, and they were involved in the **Crusades** (see pages 22–23), at times fighting on the side of the European Christians and against the Byzantines. The dynasty fell to the Mongol invasions in the 1260s.

Caravanserai

The Seljuks controlled important trade routes and set up *caravanserais*, or *khans*, about every 19 miles (31 km)—a day's travel. These were inns where traders and their camels could find food and shelter, and where goods could be stored. They were free and open to any caravan traveler. These buildings usually included rooms for people, stables for animals, water, and a mosque.

Below: The prayer room in the courtyard of the Sultanhani caravanserai in Turkey.

Islam in Spain

Al-Andalus is the Arab name for the Islamic Empire that existed in parts of present-day Spain and Portugal. From Tariq's Umayyad defeat of the Visigoths in 717, Islamic rulers held power in the region until 1492.

The Umayyads of Spain

The Muslim conquerors of al-Andalus had become divided among themselves over time. In 755, Abd al-Rahman, the Umayyad prince who had escaped during the Abbasid revolution, convinced some local leaders to back him and took control of Cordoba. He set up an independent Umayyad state with himself as *emir*, or

military leader, and began building the Great Mosque at Cordoba.

His great grandson, Abd al-Rahman II, fought off a **Viking** raid in 844 and decided to build a fleet of ships and an arsenal of weapons to repel yet other invaders. He set up a **court** that attracted important people and gained a great reputation in Europe as a center for culture and learning. In 929, Abd al-Rahman III took on the title "Caliph" at Cordoba, declaring his empire independent from the Fatimids of Cairo and the Abbasids of Baghdad.

The Almoravids

Over time, the central authority of the Umayyads broke down, and they started losing ground to the advance of Christian armies taking territory in the north of al-Andalus. The Berber kingdom of the

Above: The interior of the Christian cathedral in Cordoba shows the original red-and-white arches constructed for the mosque.

Cordoba, Spain

The court of the Umayyad rulers attracted scholars in science, math, medicine, agriculture, and the arts. Learned men of all faiths gathered in Cordoba to gain and share knowledge. From here Islamic learning spread to Europe. In 961, more than 500,000 people lived in the city.

Almoravids in Morocco decided to take action, and their ruler Yusuf ibn Tashfin crossed into al-Andalus and defeated King Alfonso VI of Leon and Castile, then took power. He introduced a version of Islam stricter than that of the previous Muslim rulers. Trade between North Africa and al-Andalus increased and this region of the Islamic Empire formed its own government and trade systems.

The Almohads

In 1147, another group of Berbers, the Almohads, replaced the Almoravids. About 1167, their ruler Abu Yusuf Ya'qub made Seville the capital. His goal, too, was to take back territory lost to the Christians. The Almohads made some gains but lost to an alliance of Christian kings in 1212 at the Battle of Las Navas de Tolosa. Cordoba fell in 1236 and the Great Mosque was converted to a Christian cathedral. Seville was taken in 1248.

Islamic rule in al-Andalus finally came to an end almost 250 years later, when Granada fell in 1492 to the Catholic monarchs Ferdinand and Isabella.

Below: On July 16, 1212, Christian forces beat the Almohads at the Battle of Las Navas de Tolosa. This was the beginning of the end for Muslim rule in al-Andalus.

19

The Fatimids

The Fatimids were Shii rulers who created an empire centered on Egypt that rivaled the Abbasids in Baghdad and the Umayyads in al-Andalus. It was a wealthy dynasty where the rulers supported the arts, science, literature, and learning. The dynasty lasted for 265 years.

Rise to Power

The Fatimids claimed to be descendants of Fatima, Muhammad's daughter and Ali's wife. They were Shii Muslims. In 909, they had taken power from the Aghlabids in North Africa. From there they moved east and took over Abbasid-controlled Egypt. In 969, they founded Cairo as a new capital. They expanded their power to the northeast and took Jerusalem and Damascus, and to the southeast where they controlled the holy cities of Mecca and Medina. They eventually lost their North African provinces west of Egypt.

Fatimid caliph Abu Mansur Nizar al-Aziz Billah ruled from 975 to 996. He organized the building of palaces, canals, bridges, and mosques. He began to use slave soldiers, or *mamluks*, in his armies.

Fighting With Saladin

The sixth Fatimid caliph, al-Hakim, ordered the destruction of the Church

Al Azhar Mosque

The al-Azhar Mosque was the first mosque built in Cairo by the Fatimids in 972. In 988 a university was started for students to learn about Shii beliefs. After the Fatimid dynasty it became a Sunni school. It is the oldest university in the world, and it is still a house of learning today.

of the Holy Sepulchre in Jerusalem in 1009. This was one of the holiest places for Christians, and this act was one reason the Christians used to justify the Crusades and to call al-Hakim the "Mad Caliph." He later became a symbol for people of the Druze faith, a mix of Islam, Judaism, and philosophy.

By the 1100s, conflicts between the Fatimids about who should be leader, problems in the army, and the invading Christian Crusaders created problems for the dynasty. The Fatimids lost control of Syria and, in 1171, it was a Sunni general, Salah al-Din, or Saladin (see pages 22–23), and his army who defeated the Christians.

In 1174, Saladin overthrew the Fatimids in Egypt and established the Ayyubid dynasty there. He eventually restored Sunni rule in Egypt.

Right: The al-Azhar Mosque in Cairo, built by the Fatimids, is an important Islamic university even today.

Below: This drawing from 1829 shows the Gate of Zuwayla in Cairo built by the Fatimids in the 1090s. The Fatmids built Cairo as a walled city with several magnificent gates.

The Crusades

The term *Crusades* is used to describe a series of wars encouraged by the Roman Catholic Church against those who were opposed to Christianity, especially Muslims. The Church felt it had to reverse Muslim advances and take control of Christian cities and holy sites such as the city of Jerusalem.

Right: A painting from about 1490 shows Saladin's forces trying to climb the outer walls of Jerusalem to capture the city.

Fight for Holy Land

The Crusaders were Christian knights, or warriors, and common people who fought on the side of the Catholic Church. The Pope, who was head of the Catholic Church, promised forgiveness of their sins to all those who helped in these wars. The Muslims called the Crusaders "the Franks" because many who fought in the First Crusade were from what is now France.

In 1071, Jerusalem was taken over by the Seljuk Turks and another Seljuk army had defeated the Byzantine Christian emperor. These Muslim military campaigns made Pope Urban II call for a crusade.

In the First Crusade, from 1096 to 1099, Christian armies took over the cities of Antioch, Jerusalem, Edessa, and Tripoli and made them the centers of small Christian states.

Muslims fought back and, in 1144, they retook Edessa. This sparked the Second Crusade and its attempt to capture the city of Damascus, but failed. Saladin conquered Egypt and, in 1187, he retook Jerusalem for Muslims. This made the Catholic Church call for a Third Crusade.

Below: These pottery tiles show the main rivals in the Third Crusade in battle, leaders Richard I "the Lionhearted" (left) and Saladin (right).

New Ideas

European Crusaders learned about Islamic culture as they traveled through Muslim lands. They saw new architecture, ate new food, and became aware of new ideas. Some Crusaders settled in the lands they conquered. Once established, Christian states in the Holy Land traded with Europe goods such as silks, textiles, precious gems, perfumes, spices, and ivory. In this way, the Crusades helped to exchange ideas between the Christians and Muslims.

The Third Crusade ended in 1192 with Richard I "the Lionhearted" of England and Saladin making a treaty, or agreement. They agreed Christian pilgrims could enter Jerusalem without paying a tribute.

The Christians were not always united in the Crusades. In 1204, Christians from the West who were supposedly on the way to fight in the Holy Land instead stopped and destroyed Byzantine Constantinople, carrying away many of its treasures.

During the rest of the Crusades, there were no major gains or losses of territory. Some Muslim leaders fought beside Crusaders against their Muslim enemies.

The Mongols

Above: This Persian miniature painting shows the Siege of Baghdad in 1258 when the Mongols led by Hulegu took it from the Abbasids.

The Mongols were a nomadic tribe from north of China that conquered most of Asia. They called their leaders *khans*. They destroyed many Muslim cities, but later converted to Islam and helped to spread Islamic beliefs and culture.

Mongols Take Over

Ghengis Khan was a powerful military leader. He invaded Central Asia and Russia and, by 1221, the cities of Samarkand and Bukhara—both centers of Islamic learning—were under his control. After his death in 1227, the Mongol Empire was split among his four sons. His son Hulagu had control over the armies in the Middle East and sacked Baghdad in Syria in 1258. His brother Chagatai was khan in Central Asia.

Right: The typical layered armor, weapon, and helmet of a Mongol warrior. The Mongols were fierce warriors who were feared by many.

A Series of Conquests

In Persia and Iraq, the Mongol invasions were devastating. The Mongols' strategy was utter ruthlessness when they captured a city so that the next city would be terrified and surrender peacefully. When Hulagu conquered Baghdad, he not only massacred much of the population but also destroyed the House of Wisdom's library. It was said that the Tigris River ran black with the ink from the books dumped into it. The Abbasid caliphate was finally ended.

The Mongols then marched into Syria, taking Damascus from the Ayyubids in 1260. At that point, the Great Khan Mongke died, and Hulagu rushed back to China. His forces in Syria were defeated by the Mamluks of Egypt to end the Mongol advance.

Reaching as Far as India

Mongol descendants remained powerful figures in the region. In 1398, Timur attacked and overthrew the Delhi Sultanate, or sultan's land, in India. He then returned to Samarkand, leaving the region in upheaval. He later defeated the Mamluks and the Ottomans. Unlike most other conquerors, Timur did not set up his own governments in the regions he conquered. This led to his empire being broken up among other forces.

While the Mongols were fierce conquerors, they opened up trade routes and enforced peace. They were also tolerant of many religions.

Gunpowder

The Mongols first learned of gunpowder when they invaded China. They brought gunpowder back with them to Muslim lands where they were the first to use it as a weapon—to propel or move a projectile.

The Mamluks

The Mamluks were Turkish slaves who were bought as boys and trained to be highly skilled soldiers. They were also taught the Sunni Muslim beliefs. They took over from the Ayyubids in Egypt, then fiercely opposed both the Mongols and the Crusaders.

Rise to Power

The practice of buying slaves to be soldiers began with the Abbasid caliphs in the 800s. This was continued with the Fatimids (900s to 1170s) as well as the Ayyubids (from 1170s) because slaves would be loyal to the sultan or caliph.

Under the Ayyubids, the Mamluks did well. Power came to the Mamluks in Egypt and Syria when Shajarat Al-Durr, widow of an Ayyubid caliph, married a Mamluk commander in 1250. In 1258, however, the Mongols under Hulagu had overtaken the Abbasids in Baghdad and were on the move toward Syria. Baybars, a Mamluk leader, led an army to Syria and defeated the Mongol army.

The Mamluks had more battles with the Mongols until the two sides signed a peace treaty in 1323. Under Baybars, the Mamluks also fought the Crusaders and took Antioch, Tripoli, and Acre. This ended the Crusades in the Holy Land.

The Mamluk Empire included the Muslim holy cities of Mecca and Medina. They traded with the Italian city-states of Venice and Genoa and with the new Ottoman Empire (see pages 38–41) centered on Bursa and Edirne. These cities were on trade routes to India and China called the Spice Route and Silk Road.

Decline and Defeat

International trade declined for the Mamluks as European ships started to sail to and from Asia for trade, bypassing their lands. In 1516, the Mamluks were defeated in Syria by the Ottomans. The battle was a bloody slaughter because the Ottomans used guns while the Mamluks did not. The Mamluk Empire was brought to an end in 1517 when Cairo was captured.

No Guns for Mamluks

When fighting the Mongols, the Mamluks did not use guns even though they had a special group of artillerymen armed with muskets. The Mamluks were skilled horsemen and preferred to fight as cavalrymen. The guns of the time could not be used on horseback and the Mamluks did not want to change their fighting methods.

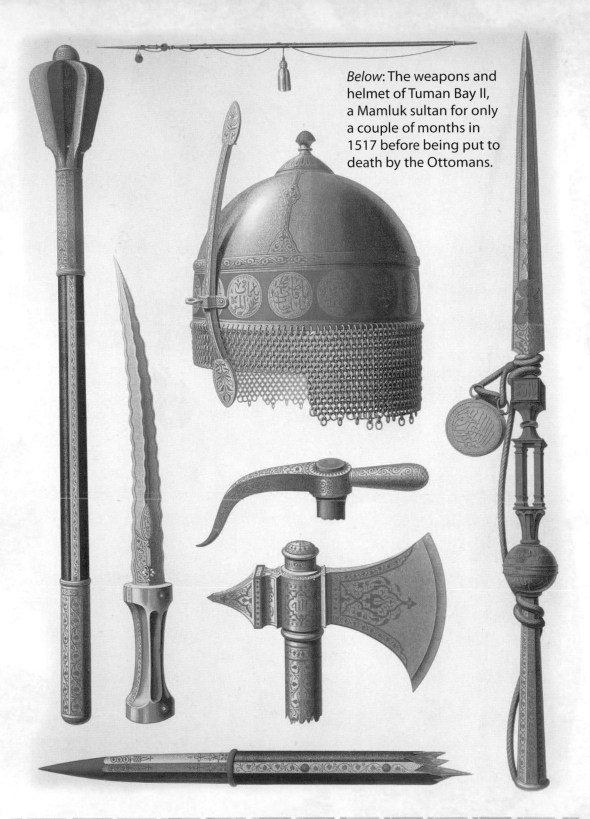

Below: The weapons and helmet of Tuman Bay II, a Mamluk sultan for only a couple of months in 1517 before being put to death by the Ottomans.

The Mughal Empire

The Mughal Empire was based in India. The Delhi Sultanate (see page 25) had established Islam in parts of northern India, and the Mughals pushed it southward. They created a large and wealthy dynasty that built many famous buildings that still exist today.

Babur's Battles

The name *Mughal* comes from the Persian word for Mongol because Timur—a Mongol—was an ancestor to Babur, the empire's founder. Babur grew up in Central Asia. In 1510, he was driven from his ancestral home of Samarkand by the Uzbeks and he went to Kabul in present-day Afghanistan to take leadership of the region. Kabul was an important trading city. Babur then moved to invade Hindustan, now known as India. He decided to use artillery, or guns, after hearing about the Ottoman victory. Babur bought the weapons from Persian and Turkish traders.

In 1526 Babur destroyed the Delhi Sultanate, which had rebuilt itself after Timur's army had destroyed it many years earlier. Babur named himself Emperor of Hindustan. However, a group of **Hindu** princes who had been planning to attack the Delhi Sultanate themselves turned to attacking Babur instead. They fought near Agra in 1526, and Babur won. This victory established the Mughal Empire.

Right: Humayun's tomb in Delhi, India, was built in 1570. The tomb is in the center of a large garden. It is the first example of Mughal garden-tomb architecture in India.

Autobiography

Babur was the first Muslim leader to write about his own life. His book is called the *Baburnama*. Babur did not explain why he wrote it all down, just that he would write the details of his life as they happened. He included both the good and bad events. He wrote in Chagatai Turkish, his native language. His book was translated into Persian in his grandson Akbar's time because, by that time, few people could read the original language.

Tumbling Down

Following Babur's death four years later, his son Humayun took over leadership of the Mughals. Babur had not established a proper government. Humayun struggled with creating law and order as well as conflicts with his brothers, each of whom wanted to be leader.

Humayun had other troubles with Sher Shah Suri, a nearby leader of Afghan background who was able to take Delhi from the Mughals. In 1555, with the help of the Shii Safavid Shah Tahmasp I, Humayun regained Delhi. Unfortunately, in 1556, Humayun died suddenly after falling down some stairs.

Above: This miniature painting from 1530 shows the Mughal Emperor Babur and his son Humayun at court.

Above: In this miniature painting from 1565, dancers perform before Emperor Akbar who is seated on a carpet.

A Golden Age

After Humayun's death, his son Akbar took the throne at only 13 years of age. By the time he was 15, he had won two battles to keep his throne. He retook all of Babur's lands and moved the capital of the empire to Agra. Akbar also expanded the empire so, by 1595, it included a large part of India. Akbar's reign is seen as the height of the Mughal Empire. He encouraged poetry, literature, science, architecture, and painting.

Akbar was also interested in other religions. He treated the Hindus well, and did not make non-Muslims pay the jizya tax. He even had several Hindu wives that he allowed to practice Hinduism. Many Hindus were given jobs as part of his government. In 1582, Akbar even started his own religion, Din-I-Ilahi, or Devine Faith. He created a new calendar that began on the date he took the throne. He had new coins stamped with the words *Allahu Akbar* that could mean either "God is Great" or "God is Akbar," but he did not make people follow his religion. Akbar died in 1605.

British Take Over

Akbar's descendants ruled the Mughal Empire for more than 100 years. When Emperor Aurangzeb died in 1707, several leaders shared power and there were revolts by Hindus and Sikhs. The empire lost more control over the region when the British beat the Mughals in battle in 1764. The British finally took control of the Indian government in 1857.

Village of Victory

Akbar moved the Mughal capital to Fatehpur Sikri, meaning "village of victory." It was 25 miles (40 km) west of Agra. The city was the Mughal capital from 1570 to 1586 before Akbar abandoned it. The red sandstone buildings made use of the area's resources. The buildings were arranged inside a 7-mile-(11-km) long wall on three sides. A lake took up the fourth side. The buildings are now a world heritage site.

Left: The Taj Mahal was built of white marble by Mughal emperor Shah Jahan, from 1631 to 1648.

The Safavids

The Safavid Empire had roots as a Sufi religious order. It became a Shii empire, making it separate from the Sunni empires of the time, the Ottomans and the Mughals. Safavid leaders were given the title *shah*, meaning king.

Early Struggles

In the late 1200s, a Sunni Sufi named Safi al-Din became leader of a large Sufi community in northwest Iran. The Safavid brotherhood was named after him. In 1501, his descendant, Ismail, became the first shah of the Safavid Empire and made Tabriz his capital city.

The Safavids battled the Ottomans to their northeast and the Uzbeks to their east. In 1508, Ismail I's forces took control of Baghdad and they won territory from the Uzbeks in Central Asia in 1510.

The Ottomans had been taxing the Qizilbash Shii Muslims living in their land so these people sided with the Safavids. It led to the Safavid and Ottoman armies meeting at the Battle of Chaldiran in 1514. The Ottoman army won, but Ismail I kept power in Persia.

Right: This miniature painting shows the Battle of Chaldiran where the Ottoman army with guns defeated the Safavid cavalry.

Right: The remains of Safavid buildings are found today at Rayan Citadel in southeast Iran. It was a walled city that included a mosque, bazaar, and stables. It was made of sunbaked mud.

Rise of Sufism

Sufis were Muslims who felt that the Sunni and Shii had moved away from being able to connect directly with God, and were too concerned with laws, rules, and rituals. Sufis focused on prayer, meditation, rhythmic chant, and even poetry. Some Sufi orders became very powerful and influential. Sufis were not interested in wealth and possessions but in living a simple life.

Ismail I made Shii Islam the Safavids' official religion. He encouraged and even forced people to convert to it. Ismail I died in 1524, and his 10-year-old son Tahmasp took over. The young shah faced revolts from the Qizilbash and threats from Uzbeks and Ottomans.

In 1533, the Ottomans retook Baghdad. In 1576, Tahmasp's brother Ismail II became shah and tried to force his people back to Sunni Islam but he was murdered. The next shah was overthrown by a Qizilbash leader in 1587, who placed the shah's son Abbas on the throne.

An Immediate Setback

Shah Abbas took the throne when he was only 16 years old. From the start of his leadership, the Qizilbash revolted. This weakened his armed forces because of the high number of Qizilbash soldiers. The Ottomans and Uzbeks took advantage of the troubles and captured the cities of Tabriz and Herat from the Safavids.

Travel Book

The French-born Sir John Chardin, or Jean-Baptiste Chardin, was a jeweler and traveler. He was a representative of the British East India Company. He is known for a ten-volume book *The Travels of Sir John Chardin in Persia and the Orient*, which was published in 1711. In it is a detailed description of the people he met and places he visited in Persia. Chardin understood the Persian language, and his book is an important record of the Safavid peoples, culture, economics, and government of the time.

Below: The Shah Mosque in Isfahan, Persia—now called Iran—built between 1611 and 1629. The building is seen as a masterpiece of Persian architecture. Its seven-color tiles were the first to be made by putting all the colors on together rather than one at a time before firing the tiles in an oven.

In 1590, Abbas signed a peace treaty with the Ottomans. Soon after, the Uzbek leader died. That allowed Abbas to settle the eastern border. In 1605, Abbas retook Tabriz and he won back Baghdad in 1623.

Great Achievements

Abbas's reign is now seen as the height of the Safavid Empire. Abbas moved the capital to Isfahan in 1598 to be farther away from his Ottoman enemies. To stop the Qizilbash revolt, Abbas started a permanent paid army. He recruited mostly non-Qizilbash people and paid them well to be loyal to him.

The Safavid court and nobles promoted a great artistic tradition in miniature painting. Trade with European countries increased under Abbas's rule. In 1616, the British East India Company agreed to trade British cloth for Persian silk. They also sold to Europe textiles and carpets made in workshops in Isfahan. The British used their navy to help Abbas defend his southern coastal borders against the Portuguese.

A Bitter End

Abbas was afraid that one of his three sons would kill him and take leadership of the empire from him as he had taken the throne from his father. As a result, in 1615, he killed one son and blinded the other two. Weak leaders ruled after Abbas, which allowed the Safavid Empire to be overrun by Afghan invaders in 1722 .

Left: A portrait of Shah Abbas I, who was also known as Abbas the Great.

Distant Empires

Other Islamic empires in Africa, Southeast Asia, China, and India added new hubs of Islamic power with their own cultural traditions.

China and Africa

Muslims first traded with China in the late 600s. Muslim scholars introduced to the Chinese inventions such as the catapult, astronomy instruments, and the lunar calendar. The Chinese exported to the Islamic world silk and **ceramics** and the secret of making paper.

Mali's Ruler

Mansa Musa ruled Mali from 1312 to 1337. In 1324 he made a pilgrimage to Mecca. This trip helped him become known far and wide because he was so wealthy. He is said to have brought with him a lot of gold, 60,000 followers, 500 slaves, and 80 camels.

Above: Putra Mosque is a modern mosque in Putrajaya, Malaysia. Today more than 60 percent of people in Malaysia are Muslim.

Right: The Great Mosque of Djenne in Mali is made of mud brick. It was built in 1907 on the site of a mosque dating from the 1200s.

In North Africa, from about 1050, the Almoravids from Morocco traded gold with the Kingdom of Ghana in West Africa across the Sahara Desert. The Kingdom of Mali eventually took over the region. Its capital Timbuktu became an important center for trading gold and salt with Europe and the Islamic Empire. King Mansa Musa made Timbuktu a major Islamic city and built mosques and madrasas there.

In the 1400s, the Songhai Empire rose to power in West Africa. Most of the Songhai rulers were Muslim, although the people followed their traditional native religion. The Songhai Empire traded with other Islamic empires such as the Mamluks in Egypt. In 1591, the kingdom ended when it was invaded by a Moroccan army.

Southeast Asia

In Southeast Asia, five different Islamic kingdoms ruled from 1206 until 1526 when they were taken over by the Mughals. Muslim traders from India first brought Islam to Sumatra. By the 1400s, the city of Malacca in Malaysia was an important trading center. Muzaffar Shah, who ruled from 1446 to 1459, declared Islam to be the state religion of Malacca. By 1470 Malacca had become the most powerful state in Southeast Asia. In 1511, the Portuguese took over Malacca. Islam later spread to many island kingdoms in what is now Indonesia.

The Ottoman Empire

The Ottoman Empire was the longest ruling Islamic empire. It lasted for more than 600 years. It rose to great power, was defeated, and rose again. The Ottomans fought against Europeans, Safavids, Mamluks, and Russians.

Origins in Turkey

By the end of the 1200s, the Turkish people had moved into Anatolia—the western half of modern Turkey. No single power ruled them. Groups of warriors followed independent leaders in battle against the Byzantines, calling themselves *ghazis*, or "warriors for the faith." They wanted to expand Muslim territories.

Janissaries

Under Orhan's rule, the Ottomans started an army made up of prisoners of war and males from conquered lands who were forced to join. They wore uniforms, were paid a salary, and were given military training to create loyalty and discipline. The soldiers were called Janissaries from the Turkish *yeni cheri* meaning "new troops." It was the first army of paid soldiers in Europe.

Osman Gazi, one of the warriors, had many victories against the Byzantines. In 1301, Osman's army overran the Byzantine Empire's former capital of Nicaea—now called Iznik— and became known as a strong military force.

Osman died in 1336 and his son Orhan took over the job of building the empire. He conquered the city of Bursa and made it the new capital. He greatly extended the state's land in Anatolia and began pushing into Europe as well.

Inroads Into Europe

Orhan's son Murad I expanded the empire farther, especially into Europe. His army took over the Balkans—a mountainous region that includes present-day Bulgaria, Romania, Serbia, and Croatia—which gave the Ottomans control of lands in Europe. At the Battle of Kosovo in 1389, they defeated the Serbian kingdom but Murad I was killed. His son Bayezid I took over expanding the Ottoman territories.

In 1402, the Ottoman state was almost destroyed. The Ottomans were defeated by Timur at the Battle of Ankara in Turkey. Bayezid was taken prisoner. He died the next year and what was left of the Ottoman territory was divided among his sons. Many regions that had been conquered by the Ottomans were lost.

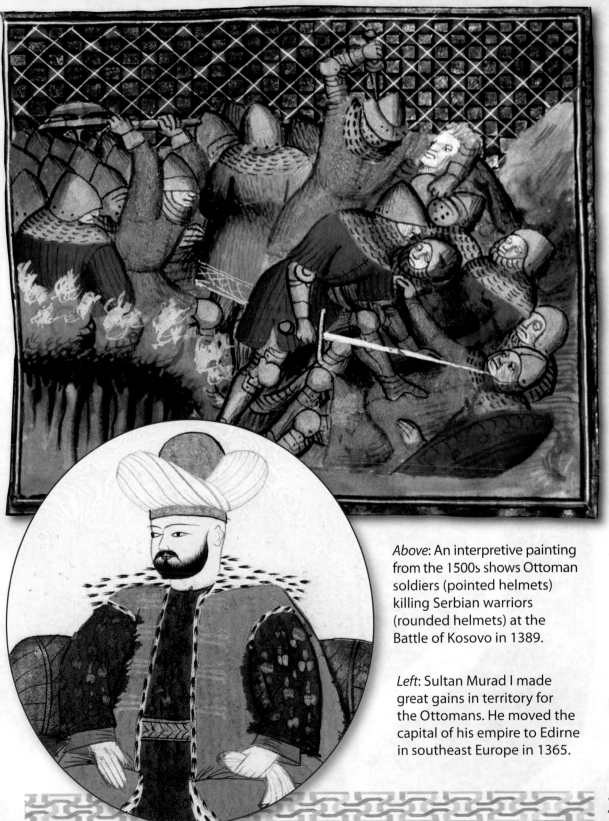

Above: An interpretive painting from the 1500s shows Ottoman soldiers (pointed helmets) killing Serbian warriors (rounded helmets) at the Battle of Kosovo in 1389.

Left: Sultan Murad I made great gains in territory for the Ottomans. He moved the capital of his empire to Edirne in southeast Europe in 1365.

Winning Back Control

The Ottomans did not stay defeated for long. After Timur died in 1405, they rebuilt their empire. One of Bayezid's sons, Mehmed I, gained power. His son, Murad II, fought to retake the Balkans. There the Ottomans saw the cannons and muskets being used by Europeans. They soon began to use the new weapons. They also built a navy after seeing Venice's navy in Italy. But it was Murad II's son, Mehmed II, who proved the Ottoman Empire's strength when he took over Constantinople in 1453 and finally ended the Byzantine Empire.

Mehmed II was called "the Conqueror" because of this and he forced many territories around the Black Sea to accept Ottoman rule. He made Istanbul his capital city. He built mosques, public buildings, baths, markets, and the famous Topkapi Palace. He turned Hagia Sophia, until then an Orthodox Christian church, into a mosque.

Reaching the Holy Cities

Under Sultan Selim, the Sunni Muslim Ottomans waged war against the Shii Muslim Safavids. In 1514, the Ottomans defeated the Safavids at the Battle of Chaldiran and gained control of Mecca and Medina.

Right: This is a helmet owned by Suleiman I "the Magnificent." It is made of brass and gold with turquoise and rubies.

Selim then fought the Mamluks, and in 1516, overtook their land and cities including Damascus, Jerusalem, and Aleppo. He killed the Mamluk sultan and claimed all of Egypt. He was given control of Mecca and Medina. This gave the Ottomans control over the holiest cities of Islam, and the Ottoman rulers added the title caliph to their name.

Suleiman I "the Magnificent" ruled after Selim. Suleiman conquered territory but also made several peace treaties. He made one such treaty with King Ferdinand of Hungary in 1533 so he could focus on fighting the Safavids. After many battles, the Safavids and Ottomans reached a peace agreement in 1555.

Escaping the Inquisition

In 1492, the Catholic monarchs Ferdinand and Isabella expelled the Jews and Muslims from Spain as part of the Inquisition. Bayezid II, son of Mehmed II, invited the refugees to settle in the Ottoman Empire and sent the Ottoman navy to escort them to their new home. Bayezid let them settle in his lands and gave them citizenship.

Below: Sultan Selim III receives government officials from parts of the Ottoman Empire at Topkapi Palace in Istanbul in about 1800.

The Last Empire

In 1536, Suleiman joined forces with King Francis I of France to stop Holy Roman emperor Charles V from taking over Europe. Suleiman also supported the **Protestant** Church to prevent the Pope from calling for a Crusade against the Ottomans. In the 1550s, he came to an agreement with Russia's Ivan IV "the Terrible" on borders between their lands. Suleiman died in 1566.

The Ottomans could no longer expand against a more powerful Europe. While its empire remained wealthy, the balance shifted, and it slowly began to lose territory to advanced European armies. The Ottoman Empire lasted until it was dissolved after World War I.

Biographies

Muhammad (570–632)

Muhammad was orphaned at an early age and raised by an Arabian merchant family. As a young man, he made several trade trips between Mecca and Palestine. He experienced what he felt were messages from God and founded the Islam religion. By the time of his death in 632, Islam had become the main religion in Arabia. After his death, the messages he received were recorded in the holy book, the Quran.

Abu Bakr (573–634)

Abu Bakr was a Meccan cloth-seller who became the first convert to Islam outside of Muhammad's family. He became Muhammad's father-in-law when his daughter Aisha married the prophet. Abu Bakr fought in early military campaigns and became the first caliph after Muhammad's death.

Umar (586–644)

A successful Meccan merchant, Umar first opposed Muhammad, at one point calling for him to be murdered. His sister, an early convert, persuaded him to take the new faith of Islam. He soon became one of Muhammad's most active helpers. Later, he became the second caliph. A great expansion of the Islamic Empire began during his caliphate.

Uthman (579–656)

A wealthy Quraysh merchant, Uthman became the fourth male to convert to Islam. His wives left him, and he married one of Muhammad's daughters. As one of Muhammad's main supporters, he became third caliph. He oversaw the first standardized written form of the Quran.

Ali (598–661)

Ali was Muhammad's cousin and played an important part in early Islam. Married to Muhammad's daughter Fatima, he became the fourth and final caliph linked to the prophet, although his caliphate was marked by strife. Shiis believe Islamic leaders should be Ali's descendants.

Muawiyah (602–680)

A relative of Uthman, Muawiyah became a convert to Islam after the capture of Mecca. He acted as Muhammad's secretary. Later, he became governor of Syria and opposed Ali. After Ali's murder, he became caliph and founded the Umayyad caliphate.

Babur (1483–1530)

Babur was a Muslim warrior and descendant of the great conqueror Genghis Khan, who founded the Mongol Empire in China, Russia, and the Middle East.

Right: Suleiman the Magnificant, sultan of the Ottoman Empire from 1520 to 1566. This painting was made by a European artist of the time.

What is known of Babur's life comes mainly from his autobiography, the *Baburnama*. In this book, he describes his early life in Central Asia and how he led an army into northern India and founded the Mughal Empire.

Suleiman I
(1495–1566)

Suleyman I was the tenth sultan of the Ottoman Empire. He was known to Europeans as "the Magnificent" because he ruled during a time when Ottoman power and culture grew. Under his rule, the Ottoman fleet controlled sea trade throughout the Persian Gulf, Mediterranean Sea, and Red Sea. He had impressive mosques built, and he supported the arts. He was known as "The Lawgiver" to his own people. He used the legal authority of the sultan to create a unified system of administration, taxation, criminal law, and land ownership.

Akbar (1542–1605)

Akbar "the Great" was just 13 when he became the third Mughal emperor of India. After winning many wars, he settled down to rule. He became famous for religious tolerance during his nearly 50-year reign, and he introduced many Hindus into his government.

Areas of Early Islamic Empires and States

Islamic control grew from its origins in Medina and Mecca during Muhammad's lifetime and spread across the Arabian peninsula. An Islamic empire was formed by Abu Bakr, the first caliph. Under Umar and Uthman, Muslim armies broke out of the peninsula and took Syria and Palestine by 638, and Egypt and the Sasanian Empire of Persia in 642. In 711, Muslim armies invaded Spain and marched as far north as central France. By 750, Muslim power extended all the way to the borders of China and India. In later centuries, the Ottoman Empire conquered southeast Europe, while traders spread Islam into East Africa.

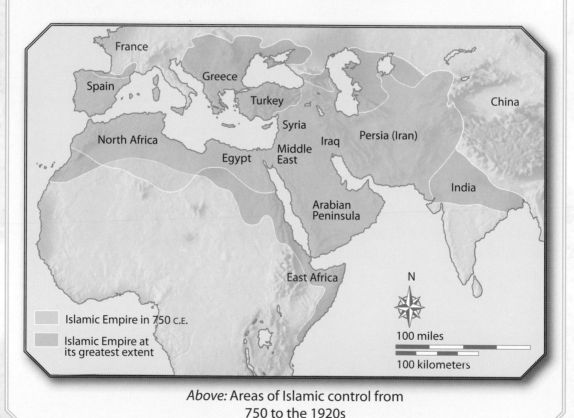

France
Greece
Spain
Turkey
China
Syria
North Africa
Middle East
Iraq
Persia (Iran)
Egypt
India
Arabian Peninsula
East Africa

N

Islamic Empire in 750 C.E.

Islamic Empire at its greatest extent

100 miles

100 kilometers

Above: Areas of Islamic control from 750 to the 1920s

Islamic World

570 Birth of Muhammad

630 Muslim conquest of Mecca

632 Death of Muhammad

633–750 Islamic caliphs and leaders invade and conquer most of the Arabian peninsula, creating the Islamic Empire

762 Baghdad becomes the capital f the Early Islamic Empire

1096–1099 First Crusade, Seljuk Turks lose Jerusalem

1187 Saladin retakes Jerusalem for Muslims

1221 Genghis Khan's Mongol armies devastate Central Asia and Persia

1260 Mamluks stop the Mongol advance

1299 Founding of the Ottoman Empire

1453 Ottoman Sultan Mehmed II overthrows Byzantine Empire and takes Constantinople

1492 Catholics reconquer Spain and expel Muslims and Jews

1526 Babur conquers India and sets up Mughal Empire

1551–1557 Suleymaniye Mosque built

1571 Battle of Lepanto between the Ottomans and Europeans ends the Islamic control over Mediterranean Sea trade

1598 Shah Abbas makes Isfahan capital of Persia

1631–1648 Taj Mahal built in Agra, India

1918–1923 Ottoman Empire collapses and is broken up

Rest of the World

793–794 Vikings start to raid Europe

800 Charlemagne crowned emperor

950s Latin manuscript in Spain introduces Islamic astrolabe and astronomy to Europe

1066 Normans conquer England

1075–1098 Earliest known Western medical treatise written by a Muslim in Italy

1096–1099 First Crusade, Christians take Jerusalem

1275–1292 Marco Polo visits China

1291 Crusades end

1405 Chinese admiral Zheng He begins first of seven voyages around Southeast Asia and the coast of Africa

1498 Vasco da Gama from Portugal sails around Africa to India

1507 Portuguese seize Hormuz at mouth of Persian Gulf

1521 Cortés conquers the Aztecs in North America

1538 Ottomans and Portuguese fight for control of Aden

1577–1580 Sir Francis Drake sails around the world

1600 British East India Company created

1789 George Washington becomes first president of the United States

Glossary

Allah The one true God of Islam; from *al* (the) *ilah* (god)

Arabia A large country in northeast Africa

bazaars Large areas where merchants buy and sell goods

Byzantines People of the empire of Byzantium, which was Christian-based and centered on Constantinople

caliphs Muslim leaders after Muhammad

caravans Groups of people and animals traveling together, usually carrying trade goods, often across a desert

ceramics Materials such as porcelain made from minerals fired in an oven

civil war Conflict between citizens, or ordinary people, living in a country

convert To change one's faith to a new religion

court A meeting place for royalty or imperial leaders and their advisors

Crusades A series of wars between European Christians and Muslims

culture The art, learning, and way of life of a people or civilization

dynasty Series of rulers from one family

empire A large area made up of different societies all ruled by one leader

Hindu Related to Hinduism, the ancient religion of India

Islam The religion or faith based on God's messages to Muhammad

Kaaba The holiest site in Islam, a square building in Mecca

madrasas Muslim places of learning, often religious schools

mosque A Muslim house of worship

Mughal A Muslim empire in India

Muslims People who follow the faith of Islam

Ottoman The Turkish Muslim empire dating from about 1517 to 1918

Persian Relating to the language or culture of Persia, now known as Iran

pilgrimage A trip taken to a holy place such as the Muslim hajj to Mecca

Protestant Relating to a branch of Christianity that broke away from the Catholic Church in Rome

Sasanid Relating to the Persian Empire or culture, which was defeated by the Muslims in 651

textiles Fabrics made by weaving fibers

traded Acting out the business of goods passing from person to person by bartering or buying and selling

translated Rewrote from one language into another

Viking Related to people from northern Europe (a region now called Scandinavia) known for raiding by sea

Visigoth People from present-day Germany who ruled Spain before the Muslims arrived

Further Information

Books

Clare, John. *Hodder History: Islamic Empires 600–1650.* London: Hodder Education, 2004.

Corzine, Phyllis. *World History Series: The Islamic Empire.* San Diego: Lucent Books, 2004.

Doak, Robin. *Great Empires of the Past: Empire of the Islamic World.* New York: Chelsea House Publishers, 2009.

Feldman, Ruth Tenzer. *Pivotal Moments in History: The Fall of Constantinople.* Minneapolis: Twenty-First Century Books, 2008.

McNeese, Tim. *Sieges that Changed the World: Constantinople.* New York: Chelsea House Publishers, 2003.

Nicolle, David. *Armies of the Caliphates: 862–1098.* London: Osprey Publishing, 1998.

Nicolle, David. *Mughul India 1504–1761.* London: Osprey Publishing, 1993.

Nicolle, David. *The Mamluks: 1250–1517.* London: Osprey Publishing, 1993.

Rumford, James. *Traveling Man: The Journey of Ibn Battuta, 1325–1354.* New York: Houghton Mifflin, 2001.

Stanley, Diane. *Saladin: Noble Prince of Islam.* New York: HarperCollins, 2002.

Wilkinson, Philip. *Islam.* New York: Dorling Kindersley, 2005.

Websites

PBS—Islam: Empire of Faith
www.pbs.org/empires/islam/

The Religion of Islam
www.religioustolerance.org/islam.htm

Muhammad: Legacy of a Prophet
www.pbs.org/muhammad/

BBC—Religions: Islam
www.bbc.co.uk/religion/religions/islam/

Index